9/08

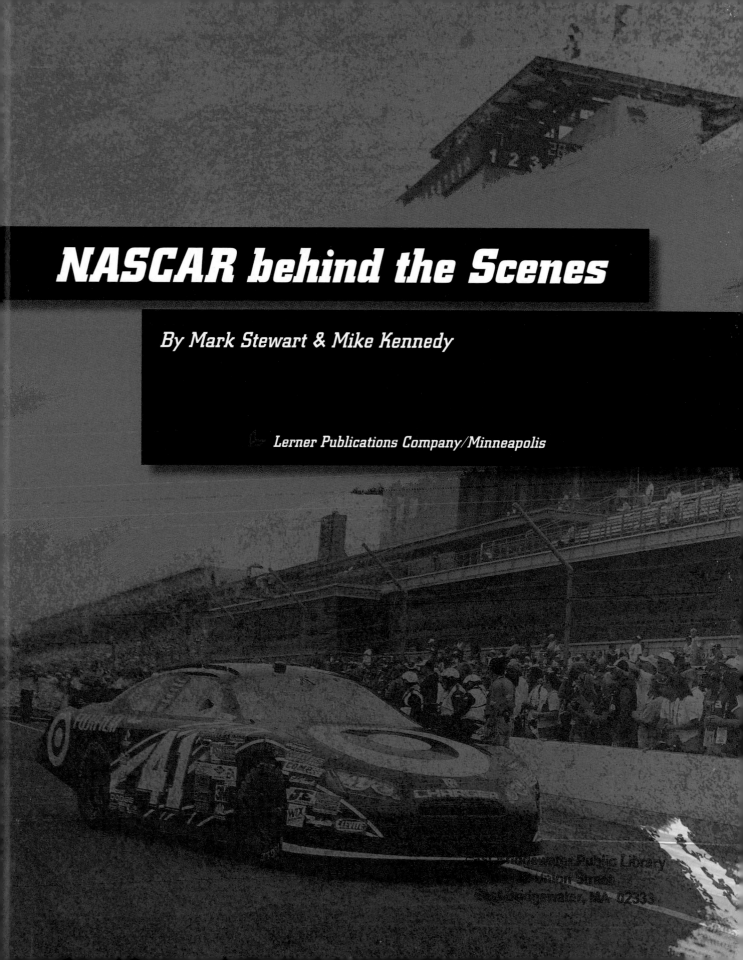

NASCAR behind the Scenes

By Mark Stewart & Mike Kennedy

Lerner Publications Company/Minneapolis

The publisher wishes to thank science teachers Amy K. Tilmont and Jeffrey R. Garside of
the Rumson Country Day School in Rumson, New Jersey, for their help in preparing this book.

Lerner Publications Company
A division of Lerner Publishing Group, Inc.
241 First Avenue North
Minneapolis, MN 55401 U.S.A.

Website address: www.lernerbooks.com

All photos provided by Getty Images.

Library of Congress Cataloging-in-Publication Data

Stewart, Mark, 1960-
NASCAR behind the scenes/by Mark Stewart & Mike Kennedy.
p. cm. -- (The science of NASCAR)
Includes index.
ISBN 978-0-8225-8743-9 (lib. bdg. : alk. paper)
1. Stock car racing—United States—Juvenile literature. 2. Pit crews—United States—Juvenile
literature. 3. NASCAR (Association)—Employees—Juvenile literature.
I. Kennedy, Mike (Mike William), 1965- II. Title.
GV1029.9.S74S747 2008
796.72—dc22   2007035031

Manufactured in the United States of America
1 2 3 4 5 6 – DP – 13 12 11 10 09 08

Contents

Introduction

Have you ever wondered what working at a NASCAR race would be like? Thousands of people get to live this dream every year. They work behind the scenes to help NASCAR races run smoothly. Some people have jobs that bring them close to the action for just a few days. For others, working at races is a year-round job.

GREEN MEANS GO! A NASCAR OFFICIAL TELLS DRIVERS TO START RACING.

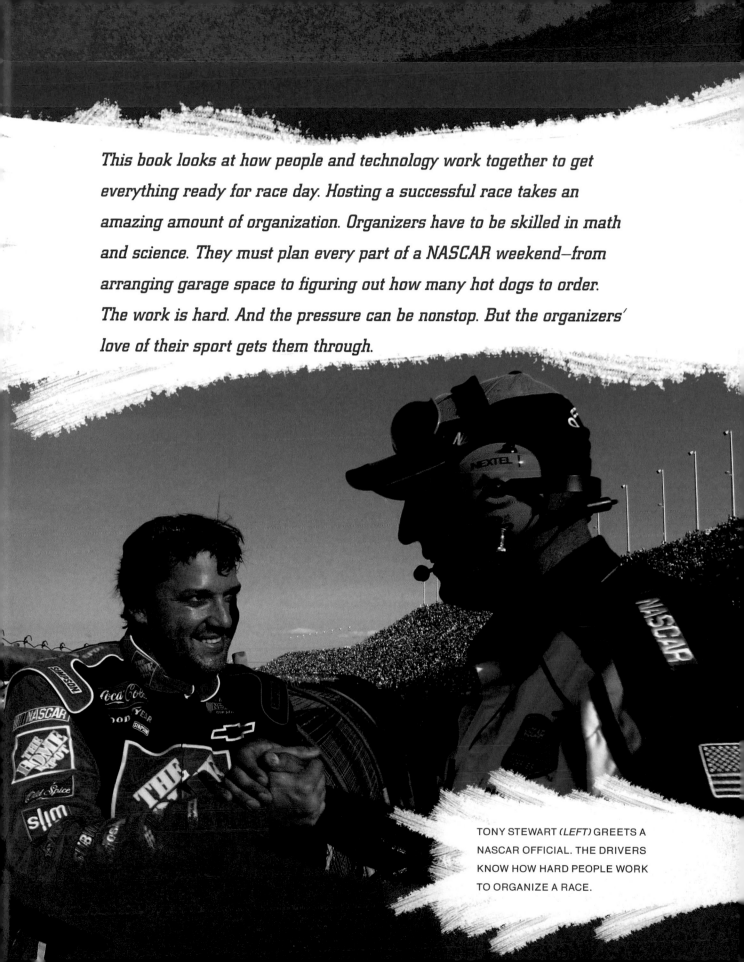

This book looks at how people and technology work together to get everything ready for race day. Hosting a successful race takes an amazing amount of organization. Organizers have to be skilled in math and science. They must plan every part of a NASCAR weekend—from arranging garage space to figuring out how many hot dogs to order. The work is hard. And the pressure can be nonstop. But the organizers' love of their sport gets them through.

TONY STEWART *(LEFT)* GREETS A NASCAR OFFICIAL. THE DRIVERS KNOW HOW HARD PEOPLE WORK TO ORGANIZE A RACE.

Chapter One: Making Races Happen

NASCAR people are good at what they do. They have to be. Fans and racing teams depend on them. Races just don't happen by themselves. In many cases, the planning starts years before the race is scheduled.

The first step for most races is to find a sponsor. A sponsor is a company that pays to put its name on a race. For example, the Coca-Cola 600 is a race that has a soft-drink company as its main sponsor. Companies like to be connected to winning. If a company sponsors one car, the company has only one chance to win. By sponsoring a whole race, a company is guaranteed to be part of the victory celebration.

BANK OF AMERICA
SPONSORS THIS RACE
AT LOWE'S MOTOR SPEEDWAY
IN NORTH CAROLINA.

Do the Math

The number next to a race's name tells you how long it is in miles, not in laps. The Bank of America 500 is held at a track that is two miles around. How many laps is this race?

(answer on page 48)

TOP: TWO FAMOUS DRIVERS, RICHARD PETTY (LEFT) AND JEFF GORDON, POSE IN FRONT OF THE SIGN FOR THE 2007 PEPSI 500. ABOVE: BOBBY LABONTE CELEBRATES A VICTORY IN FRONT OF THE RACE SPONSOR'S SIGN.

Dollars and Sense

All drivers race to win. A victory earns big money. Each race on the NASCAR schedule puts aside prize money for the drivers. Sponsors supply much of the money and the winner's trophy. For example, a company that sells car insurance sponsors the Allstate 400. The winner of the 2007 Allstate 400 was Tony Stewart. He won almost $500,000.

JEFF GORDON IS HAPPY AFTER HE WINS A 2007 RACE AND SO IS DUPONT, GORDON'S MAIN SPONSOR. DUPONT MAKES PAINT FOR CARS.

At the 2007 Daytona 500, Kevin Harvick won $1.5 million for finishing first. Mark Martin won $1.1 million for finishing second. Stewart, who finished last, still won more than $300,000. The Daytona 500 is NASCAR's richest race.

TONY STEWART DOESN'T ALWAYS TAKE HOME A TROPHY. BUT WITH PRIZE MONEY FROM SPONSORS, HE EARNS SOMETHING FOR EVERY RACE HE FINISHES.

Do the Math

Let's say the winning driver in a race receives $350,000. The last-place driver receives $50,000. What is the difference in prize money between first and last place?

(answer on page 48)

Sell! Sell! Sell!

As race day nears, organizers must start selling tickets. Fans can buy tickets for practice runs, qualifying runs, and race day. NASCAR does a good job of giving fans information on future races. The organization lets fans know how to get tickets. In recent years, more and more fans are buying their tickets on the Internet.

Fans also buy souvenirs when they come to a race. Thousands of caps, T-shirts, photos, toy cars, and trading cards must be ordered beforehand. NASCAR fans love to show their support for their favorite drivers. They buy items that have the name, car number, and driver's face on them. The souvenir vendors have to guess who's hot and who's not months before a race.

RACING FANS SHOW THEIR LOYALTY TO
THEIR FAVORITE DRIVERS IN MANY WAYS.

Do the Math

A vendor with Kevin
Harvick souvenirs sells
twice as many caps as
T-shirts in an afternoon.
Let's say the vendor
sold 200 caps. How
many shirts were sold?

(answer on page 48)

See for Yourself

You will notice a lot of signs for soft drinks at a NASCAR race. The fizzy soft drinks have had a gas called carbon dioxide put in them. This is why these beverages are called carbonated. How does the carbon dioxide escape from soda? To find out, try this experiment.

- Using a measuring cup, divide a 16-ounce bottle of soda in half.
- Leave eight ounces in the bottle. Empty the other eight ounces into a large plastic cup.
- Screw the cap tightly onto the bottle.
- Let the two containers sit for 48 hours. (Each time a bubble rises to the surface of the soda, a small amount of carbon dioxide is escaping.)
- Take a sip of the soda in the cup. You'll see that it's flat. This means it has lost its carbonation. But what about the soda in the bottle?
- Unscrew the cap and taste the soda. It's flat too!

The bottled soda went flat because its carbon dioxide fit into the empty eight ounces of space at the top of the bottle. The pffft sound you heard when you unscrewed the cap was the gas escaping all at once.

Drivers Unite!

BILL FRANCE SR.

In the 1930s and 1940s, stock car racing was just beginning. Race track owners were not always honest. Drivers paid a fee to enter a race and got prize money if they won. When the winning drivers came for their cash, sometimes the owners had driven off with it!

To fix this problem, Bill France Sr. started the National Association of Stock Car Auto Racing (NASCAR) in 1947. He wanted to make sure that drivers were treated fairly. He also wanted fans to see the best racing possible. NASCAR used the same rules at every race. The organization made a schedule that everyone could follow.

Shoptalk

"FRANCE GOT INVOLVED WHEN THIS BUSINESS WAS AS ROUGH AND TOUGH A SPORT AS THERE WAS."

–HUMPY WHEELER, NASCAR PIONEER *(LEFT)*

In the weeks and months before a race, NASCAR workers have a long list of things that must get done. They are responsible for the safety and comfort of everyone who comes to the race. One of the most important jobs is to look at the track very closely.

During cold months, the surface of a track shrinks slightly. On hot days, the track expands slightly. Why does this happen? The road surface is made up of atoms (very tiny parts). As the temperature rises, the atoms move faster. They take up more space, so the surface gets bigger. In cold weather, the atoms slow down. They take up less space, so the track gets smaller. Shrinking and expanding can cause the track to crack and buckle, especially where sections of track meet. Workers must repair the problems before any racing can be done.

A WORKER REPAIRS A CRACK AT MARTINSVILLE SPEEDWAY IN VIRGINIA.

In the Mix

On qualifying day, cars run two laps as fast as they can. The cars making the fastest qualifying runs get the best starting spots on race day. Many drivers feel lucky when they go last during qualifying. Why? The track is cooler in the late afternoon than at midday. A cooler track can help a car go a little faster because the tires get a better grip.

NASCAR PRESIDENT MIKE HELTON *(CENTER)* AND TWO OTHER NASCAR OFFICIALS LOOK OVER THE TRACK AT BRISTOL MOTOR SPEEDWAY IN TENNESSEE.

You're Hired

In the months between races, most tracks only need a few dozen workers. When NASCAR comes to town, they need hundreds. At some races, more than 100,000 fans jam into the track in just a few hours. People need to help them park. Others have to show them to their seats. Vendors sell them food, beverages, and souvenirs. Workers clean up after them.

A TRACK WORKER REPAINTS THE WALL AT DARLINGTON RACEWAY IN SOUTH CAROLINA.

Some people at the race are employees of NASCAR. They travel to the various tracks throughout the year. However, most of the workers live in towns near the track. This includes the security and safety crews. Security guards make sure that fans don't endanger themselves or others. Safety crew members help drivers and their teams in case an accident occurs. These workers are often firefighters and emergency workers from nearby towns.

Do the Math

Let's say a track pays workers $15 an hour. A worker starts at 8:00 A.M. on race day and finishes at 8:00 P.M. How much will that worker earn?

(answer on page 48)

Pedigree

A WORKER TAKES CARE OF THE ENTRANCE TO THE PARKING LOT AT THE DAYTONA INTERNATIONAL SPEEDWAY IN FLORIDA.

Do the Math

A NASCAR official lives 320 miles from a track. The owner of the same track lives 10 miles away. How much farther must the official travel to the race than the track owner?

(answer on page 48)

On the Air

Before a race, skilled technicians make sure everything is ready for the TV, radio, and Internet hookups that bring the action to the fans. They set up TV cameras on high platforms. Cables connect the cameras to a set of TV screens. A director chooses the shots that viewers will see.

JAMIE LITTLE OF ESPN (*RIGHT*) INTERVIEWS DRIVER ROBBY GORDON. HER WIRELESS EQUIPMENT LETS HER MAKE BROADCASTS FROM ALMOST EVERY PART OF THE TRACK.

RIGHT: EVERY NASCAR TRACK HAS A SPECIAL STAND FOR TV CAMERAS.

Fewer cables and wires are at a NASCAR race than in years past. Wireless technology brings TV cameras close to the action. It also powers laptop computers and handheld devices.

In a Flash

Fans and race teams depend on wireless technology during a race. They must make sure that no thick walls or pillars stand between them and the source of the signal. Blocking the signal can slow down the speed of their computers.

ABOVE: AN ARTIST FINISHES A PAINTING FOR THE NASCAR SPRINT CUP SERIES. SPRINT IS A LARGE WIRELESS TECHNOLOGY COMPANY.

See for Yourself

TV and Internet signals travel very fast. They are too fast to measure for yourself. However, you can test the speed of sound. Try this experiment. (Make sure you do the experiment outdoors.)

- Ask permission to get a bathroom hand towel wet.
- Twirl the ends of the wet towel lengthwise in your hands. Make sure the towel has wrapped around itself as far as it will go. (Be sure no one is in front of you.)
- Snap the towel forward and backward quickly. (Use the same arm motion as you would if you were throwing a flying disc.)
- Keep trying until you hear a loud crack.

For an instant, the end of the wet towel has moved the air faster than the speed of sound. The cracking sound is called a sonic boom (explosion of sound). The speed of sound is 769 miles per hour. This is about four times faster than the usual speed of a NASCAR racing car.

Wheel Deal

Race cars use more than 1,000 tires at most NASCAR events. Thousands more tires must be available in case track conditions change. Tires are big and bulky. Luckily, the teams don't have to move them. The tires are waiting at the track when the teams arrive. The Goodyear Tire and Rubber Company supplies NASCAR with all of its tires. Goodyear is in charge of bringing tires—and tire specialists—to all NASCAR races.

Shoptalk

"HAVING A SEPARATE COMPANY DEAL WITH THE WHEELS MAKES IT EASIER."

—DRIVER MARK MARTIN

ABOVE: A WORKER STACKS GOODYEAR TIRES BEFORE A RACE AT MICHIGAN INTERNATIONAL SPEEDWAY. *LEFT:* MARK MARTIN AND OTHER DRIVERS LIKE HAVING ONE COMPANY SUPPLY ALL THE TIRES FOR A RACE.

Chapter Three: On the Move

NASCAR fans often say a day at the track is a moving event. For the people who race for a living, every week is a moving event! Only 43 cars are allowed to start each race. Add 150,000 fans, and you have a lot of people to move in and out.

For drivers and their crews, moving in actually begins with moving out. Most races are only a week apart. So teams don't have much time to get from one track to the next. When a race is over, every crew member becomes a professional mover. They pack and go!

TEAM MEMBERS LOAD THE CARS OF TONY STEWART (NO. 20) AND CARL EDWARDS (NO. 99) INTO HAULERS AFTER A RACE.

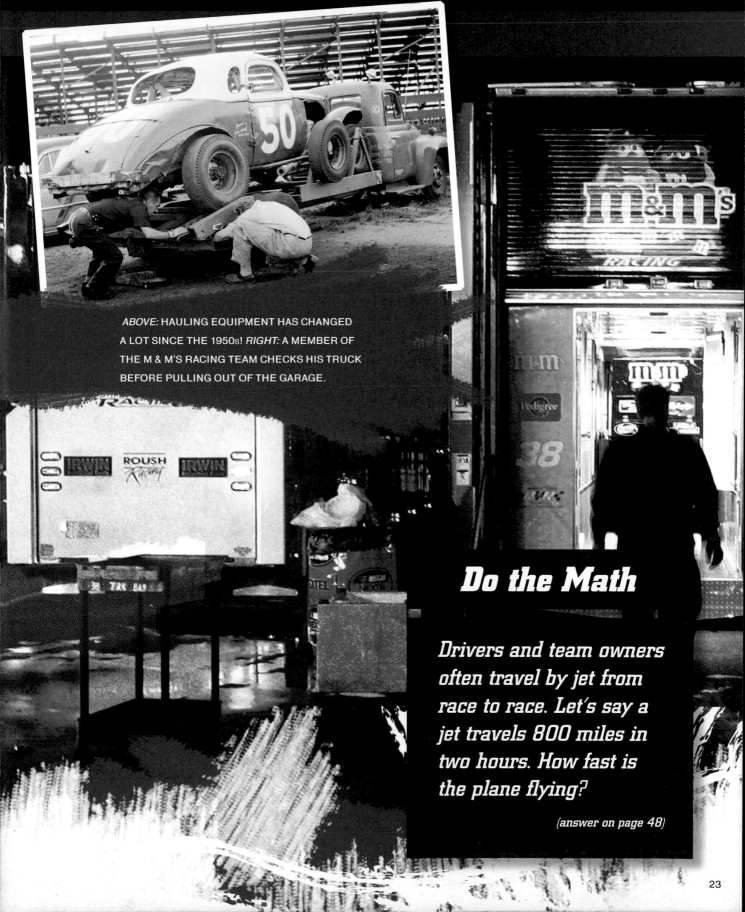

ABOVE: HAULING EQUIPMENT HAS CHANGED A LOT SINCE THE 1950s! *RIGHT:* A MEMBER OF THE M & M'S RACING TEAM CHECKS HIS TRUCK BEFORE PULLING OUT OF THE GARAGE.

Do the Math

Drivers and team owners often travel by jet from race to race. Let's say a jet travels 800 miles in two hours. How fast is the plane flying?

(answer on page 48)

The Long Drive

How does a NASCAR team get all of its cars, engines, equipment, and people to the next race in just a couple of days? They depend on several big vehicles, including haulers and motor homes. The drivers of these vehicles are almost as important to their teams as the race car drivers. They often become mechanics or members of the pit crew after the cars are unloaded.

TOP: NASCAR TRUCKS ARE MADE SO CARS AND EQUIPMENT CAN BE STACKED. *ABOVE:* JEFF GORDON'S TRUCK HEADS FOR THE HIGHWAY.

By Design

The inside of a NASCAR hauler is an amazing place. Everything a mechanic needs is in here. It is like a garage on wheels.

NASCAR haulers use the same colors and designs as the cars they carry. They can be seen rumbling down the highway early each week. They have become very popular with fans. Some of the best-selling NASCAR souvenirs are the toy versions of the haulers.

MICHAEL WALTRIP'S CAR IS INSIDE THIS NAPA HAULER.
THE TRUCK IS PAINTED WITH THE SAME COLORS AS HIS CAR.

Here They Come!

What is involved in getting thousands of NASCAR fans from their homes to their seats at the track? The cities and towns that hold NASCAR races spend as much time preparing as the race workers do. The police must be ready to handle 50,000 extra cars. Hotels and motels have to hire more workers. And restaurants had better not run out of food!

THE FANS RISE TO THEIR FEET FOR THE START OF A RACE AT LOWE'S MOTOR SPEEDWAY. IT TAKES A LOT OF PLANNING AND HARD WORK TO GET SO MANY PEOPLE IN AND OUT OF A TRACK.

Some fans bring their food and beds with them. They arrive in campers and motor homes. They find a spot with a good view of the track. They stay for practice runs, qualifying runs, and the race. They cook all of their meals there. They sit on top of their vehicles and watch the action. They claim to have the best seats in the house.

THESE FANS BELIEVE THEY HAVE
THE BEST SEATS IN THE HOUSE!

Do the Math

The stands at NASCAR races can get hot. Let's say each person in a family of four gulps down two quarts of beverages during a race. How many gallons will they drink altogether?

(answer on page 48)

See for Yourself

The more time you spend on the road, the better you get at judging speed and distance. The next time you are on a long car ride, try this experiment.

- Ask the driver to tell you exactly when the odometer starts a new mile.
- While this part is going on, look out the window of the car. Count as evenly as you can.
- The driver should tell you exactly when the mile is done. Write down the number you reach when one mile is completed.
- Wait a few minutes. Look out the window again. Try to decide whether you are moving a little faster, a little slower, or the same speed.
- Based on this guess, jot down a number. This is your guess of how long the next mile will take.
- Ask the driver to let you know about the start and finish of the next mile.
- How close was your guess?

This is actually a fun driving game. If you want to play against another passenger, use a watch as a timer so that the counting is fair for both players.

Fueling Up

NASCAR teams don't have to move fuel from race to race. This would be difficult and dangerous. The fuel comes to the track in large tanker trucks. Often pictures of NASCAR drivers are on the side. For many years, NASCAR's fuel had lead in it. Lead added to gas makes an engine perform better. But leaded fuel is bad for us and the environment. NASCAR tested cleaner fuels for many years. It finally found one that worked. In 2008, NASCAR started using cleaner, unleaded fuel at all of its races.

SUNOCO BEGAN SUPPLYING CLEANER FUEL TO NASCAR IN 2008.

Do the Math

Let's say tanker trucks bring 5,000 gallons of fuel to a NASCAR race. The race teams use 4,800 gallons. How much is left?

(answer on page 48)

Chapter Four: In the Garage

The busiest part of a NASCAR race track is the infield. This area is inside the oval. The busiest part of the infield is the garage area. This is where the racing teams work, beginning the day the haulers arrive. NASCAR garages are very crowded. More than 40 cars and their crews must squeeze into tight working spaces.

NASCAR garages have all the things that mechanics need. Hydraulic lifts raise the cars off the ground. Hoses with pressurized air create power for different tools. Shelves and racks hold tires and other equipment. Computers and testing equipment are plugged into electric outlets. Before a race, drivers relax in the garage area. It's like the locker room in other sports.

THERE IS NOT A LOT OF ROOM IN A NASCAR GARAGE. JUST A FEW FEET SEPARATE THE CARS OF JIMMIE JOHNSON (NO. 48), JEFF GORDON (NO. 24), AND MATT KENSETH (NO. 17).

Do the Math

Everyone on a NASCAR team works hard. Let's say a team member works 10 hours a day for six days, then gets a day off. How many hours has the person worked during that week?

(answer on page 48)

GASOLINE ALLEY AT THE INDIANAPOLIS MOTOR SPEEDWAY IN INDIANA IS ONE OF THE MOST FAMOUS GARAGES IN RACING.

Decisions, Decisions

The star of the garage area is each team's race car. Each NASCAR track is a little different. So the team must make many decisions every week. What kind of suspension system should be used? How much air pressure in tires will work best on the track's surface? How can the engine be tweaked to give the most power during the race?

MECHANICS WORK ON JEFF BURTON'S CAR BETWEEN
PRACTICE RUNS FOR THE 2007 USG SHEETROCK 400
AT CHICAGOLAND SPEEDWAY IN ILLINOIS.

A racing team's engineers, mechanics, and specialists try different ways of solving these problems. Practice runs give them a chance to see how each idea works. After each practice run, the driver pulls back into the garage. The crew members talk about what is and isn't working. Sometimes one team has two or three cars running. The crew chiefs, who are in charge of each car, can share this information. This is why many owners like to have more than one car in a race.

By Design

NASCAR doesn't allow a race team to change the shape of its car. NASCAR officials use aluminum templates (patterns) to check. A car must fit inside the template to be allowed to race.

ABOVE LEFT: A NASCAR CREW MAKES CHANGES TO BOTH ENDS OF A CAR AT THE SAME TIME. *ABOVE RIGHT:* DRIVER PAUL MENARD *(LEFT)* CHECKS THE RESULTS FROM A PRACTICE RUN.

Crowd Control

NASCAR fans have always liked getting close to their favorite cars and drivers. Sometimes they get too close! Crew members have to squeeze past fans as they work on different parts of a car. Sometimes fans are bumped by cars or hit by equipment.

RACING FANS FILL THE GARAGE AREA AT THE DAYTONA INTERNATIONAL SPEEDWAY.

A few years ago, NASCAR decided to limit the number of people who got to go behind the scenes. Special passes are needed to visit the infield and garage areas. This is for the safety of the racing teams and the fans. For people who love to watch the experts at work, some tracks have installed garage cameras. They show fans what's going on, even if they can't be close to the action.

DRIVER KASEY KAHNE SIGNS AUTOGRAPHS FOR FANS AT LAS VEGAS MOTOR SPEEDWAY IN NEVADA.

Do the Math

Let's say 500 garage passes are issued on qualifying day. Another 1,500 are issued on race day. How many people get behind the scenes during those two days?

(answer on page 48)

See for Yourself

Compressed air runs several tools in a NASCAR garage. A compressor creates pressure on air by squeezing it into a small space. When the air is allowed to escape through a hose, the tool on the other end gets a big burst of power. To understand how this works, try this experiment.

- Find two balloons. One should be small, the other large.
- Blow up the large balloon with five full breaths. Pinch the end to prevent air from escaping.
- Mark a spot on the floor. Let go of the balloon at that spot. Measure the distance the balloon travels.
- Blow up the small balloon with five full breaths. Repeat the experiment. The smaller balloon will travel farther (and faster!).

Your five breaths squeezed the same amount of air into both balloons. But the smaller balloon had less space. The air was compressed inside the balloon. The pressure you created in the small balloon gave it a more powerful flow. This is how air compressors make the power for tools such as the air guns that loosen and tighten lug nuts on tires.

In the Shop

Every garage is the same at a NASCAR race. But not all year-round race car garages, or shops, are equal. Between seasons—and sometimes between races—a lot of work goes on in a team's shop. Owners who can afford the best equipment give their teams a big advantage. One of the best machines is a seven-post shaker rig. This machine tests how a car's suspension system and its frame will hold up during a race. The rig shakes the car with the same powerful forces that a car feels during a race.

TONY STEWART'S CARS ARE A TOP PRIORITY IN THE JOE GIBBS RACING GARAGE.

Shoptalk

"THREE-FOURTHS OF A RACE IS WON IN THE GARAGE."

—DRIVER LEE PETTY (*LEFT*), WINNER OF THE FIRST DAYTONA 500

Chapter Five: Race Day

Before a race begins, NASCAR teams move from their garage area to the pits. This is where a car stops for refueling, new tires, and minor repairs. Drivers exit the track by way of pit road to get to their pit crews. A safety wall separates pit road from the rest of the track. Cars must enter the pits at low speeds—usually between 35 and 55 miles per hour. If drivers go too fast, they can be penalized. They may have to pay money, or they may lose time.

Do the Math

Let's say a pit crew changes all four tires five times during a race. What is the total number of tires they use?

(answer on page 48)

REED SORENSON DRIVES DOWN PIT ROAD AT THE INDIANAPOLIS MOTOR SPEEDWAY.

Each team has its own box and stall on pit road. Yellow lines mark the pit boxes. When a driver pulls into the pit box, seven team members from the pit stall hop over the safety wall. Four people change the tires. Two people add more fuel to the car. One person operates the jack that lifts the car for the tire changers.

ABOVE: CARS PULL IN AND OUT OF THE PITS DURING A RACE AT CHICAGOLAND SPEEDWAY. *ABOVE RIGHT:* TONY STEWART'S PIT CREW MUST DECIDE QUICKLY WHETHER HIS CAR IS TOO DAMAGED TO KEEP RACING.

To the Rescue

Sometimes a race is interrupted. This can happen when car parts stray onto the track or when an accident happens. Drivers are told about the interruption on their radios. A NASCAR official waves a yellow caution flag. This is the signal for all drivers to slow down. NASCAR officials then tell safety crews when it is safe to go on the track. For the next few minutes, safety crew members do their jobs.

In some cases, a car has stopped working altogether. The car can't be driven anymore. NASCAR's rules say that its driver must ride an ambulance to the treatment center in the infield. Here a team of three doctors and four nurses check the driver for injuries. They send injured drivers to a local hospital.

EVEN IF DRIVERS ARE UNHURT, NASCAR RULES SAY THEY MUST TAKE AN AMBULANCE RIDE TO THE INFIELD CARE CENTER IF THEIR CARS CAN NO LONGER BE DRIVEN.

Flying Colors

NASCAR signals drivers with a series of flags. What do they mean?

- Green means go. Drivers can start racing at full speed.
- Yellow means drive with caution. No passing is allowed during a caution period.
- Red means stop. The track is too unsafe to drive.
- Black means go to the pits. Drivers are black-flagged when their car is badly damaged or they have broken the rules.
- Blue with a yellow stripe means let another driver pass. Slower cars sometimes see this flag.
- White means the lead car has one lap to go.
- The checkered flag means the winner has crossed the finish line.

THE RED FLAG CAME OUT AFTER JEFF GORDON'S ACCIDENT IN THE 2007 COCA-COLA 600. HIS CAR HAD TO BE TOWED OFF THE TRACK.

Make It Official

Race officials do more than direct safety crews. NASCAR has a lot of rules to make racing fair and safe. Officials enforce these rules from the moment a car rolls into the garage area. They check cars again and again, even after the race is over.

A NASCAR OFFICIAL SIGNALS TO JEFF GORDON.
DRIVERS MUST FOLLOW THE INSTRUCTIONS OF THE
OFFICIALS AT ALL TIMES.

Sometimes during a race, NASCAR officials must decide when to slow down cars. If they see an unsafe situation, they tell the flag official to wave the yellow caution flag. At this moment, no more passing is allowed. Cars are frozen in order. Drivers with big leads don't like yellow flags. Even though the cars behind the leader can't pass, they can bunch up right behind the leader before the race is restarted.

ABOVE LEFT: A NASCAR OFFICIAL *(LEFT)* TALKS TO DRIVER J. J. YELEY BEFORE A QUALIFYING RUN. *ABOVE RIGHT:* A NASCAR OFFICIAL TELLS DRIVERS THERE ARE THREE LAPS TO GO DURING A RACE AT THE TEXAS MOTOR SPEEDWAY IN FORT WORTH.

See for Yourself

When a race begins again after a caution period, there is a mad dash for first place. The lead car must get up to speed the instant the race is restarted. Otherwise the other drivers can speed right past the leader. To understand why timing is so important, try this experiment.

- Gather four of your friends. Ask them to compete in a short race.
- Mark a starting line and a finish line about 20 feet apart.
- Have two runners begin on the starting line, two arm lengths apart. Have the two others stand in between them but one big step behind the front two.
- Stand at the finish line. Tell the runners they can start the instant they hear you say the word *cat*.
- Say a couple of different words, such as *dog* and *fish*, before saying *cat*. This keeps the racers from leaving too early.
- Run this race several times. Notice that the front two runners often don't finish ahead of the back two runners.

These races are just like NASCAR restarts. It doesn't always matter where you start from. It's more important to get a great start.

Playing by the Rules

NASCAR has rules for almost everything. If someone breaks the rules, NASCAR can punish the driver with fines and other penalties. Drivers also have a set of rules. They don't mind driving hard, but they will not stand for unsafe driving. The more NASCAR races you watch, the more you will see how drivers police one another.

Shoptalk

"RUBBING TO GET BY SOMEBODY IF THEY'RE PINCHING YOU DOWN...THAT'S NOT ROUGH—THAT'S RACING!"

—DRIVER DALE EARNHARDT SR.

TOP: TWO DRIVERS ARGUE AFTER AN ACCIDENT AT WATKINS GLEN, NEW YORK. UNSAFE DRIVING MAKES THESE COMPETITORS VERY ANGRY. *LEFT:* NO ONE KNEW NASCAR'S RULES OF THE ROAD BETTER THAN DALE EARNHARDT SR.

Glossary

hauler: a vehicle that takes a NASCAR team from race to race

hydraulic lift: a machine that uses the power of fluids in motion to raise a car high off the ground

lap: one circuit around a track; to be ahead of another car by one entire circuit of the track

pit crew: the seven-member team that takes care of a race car during a race. The crew chief leads the pit crew.

practice run: a period of time given to each team to test its car on the track

qualifying run: the chance given to each car to drive two laps as fast as possible. The faster the qualifying run, the better the starting spot on race day.

sonic boom: a noise made by the shock wave of an object traveling faster than the speed of sound

sponsor: the group or person who pays money to support a race or racing team

suspension system: the springs, shocks, and other parts that are used to suspend (hang) a car's frame, body, and engine above the wheels

template: an aluminum pattern used to check the size and shape of different parts of a race car

vendor: a person who sells something to fans at the track

wireless technology: the passing of electronic signals through the air

Learn More

Books

Buckley, James. *NASCAR*. New York: DK Eyewitness Books, 2005.

Buckley, James. *Speedway Superstars*. Pleasantville, NY: Reader's Digest, 2004.

Doeden, Matt. *Stock Cars*. Minneapolis: Lerner Publications Company, 2007.

Fielden, Greg. *NASCAR Chronicle*. Lincolnwood, IL: Publications International, Ltd., 2003.

Savage, Jeff. *Dale Earnhardt Jr*. Minneapolis: Lerner Publications Company, 2006.

Sporting News. *NASCAR Record & Fact Book*. Charlotte, NC: Sporting News, 2007.

Woods, Bob. *The Greatest Races*. Pleasantville, NY: Reader's Digest, 2004.

Woods, Bob. *NASCAR Pit Pass: Behind the Scenes of NASCAR*. Pleasantville, NY: Reader's Digest, 2005.

Website and Video Game

NASCAR
http://www.nascar.com
NASCAR.com is the official site of NASCAR. From here you can find information on drivers and their teams, as well as previews of upcoming races, schedules, and a look back at NASCAR's history.

NASCAR 2008. Video game. Redwood City, CA: EA Sports, 2008.
With an ESRB rating of E for "everyone," this game gives fans a chance to experience the speed and thrills of driving in a NASCAR race.

Index

Do the Math Answers

Page 7: 250 laps. 500 miles ÷ 2 miles per lap = 250 laps.

Page 9: $300,000. $350,000−$50,000=$300,000.

Page 11: 100 T-shirts. 0.5 x 200 caps = 100 shirts.

Page 16: $180. 12 hours x $15 = $180.

Page 17: 310 miles. 320 miles−10 miles = 310 miles.

Page 23: 400 miles per hour. 800 miles ÷ 2 hours = 400 miles per hour.

Page 27: 2 gallons. 4 quarts = 1 gallon.
2 quarts x 1 person = 2 quarts. 8 quarts = 8 people. 8 quarts x 4 people = 2 gallons.

Page 29: 200 gallons. 5,000 gallons − 4,800 gallons = 200 gallons.

Page 31: 60 hours. 10 hours x 6 days = 60 hours.

Page 35: 2,000 people. 1,500 passes + 500 passes = 2,000 passes for 2,000 people.

Page 38: 24 tires. 4 tires x 5 changes = 20, 20 + 4 original tires = 24 tires used.

48